The Language of Yes is Kevin Crossley-Holland's first collection of verse since his *New and Selected Poems 1965–90*. He is the author of new versions of *The Norse Myths* and translator of *The Anglo-Saxon World*, including Beowulf, and *The Exeter Book Riddles*, while his many books for children include *Beowulf, British Folk Tales* and the Carnegie Medal-winning *Storm*. He has collaborated with a number of composers, including Nicola LeFanu, with whom he has written two operas: *The Green Children* and *The Wildman*, which was given its première at the Aldeburgh Festival in 1995.

Crossley-Holland has recently returned to England from Minnesota, where he was Fulbright Visiting Scholar at St Olaf College in 1990 and Endowed Chair in the Humanities and Fine Arts at the University of St Thomas 1991–95.

Poetry by the same author

COLLECTIONS

The Rain–Giver
The Dream–House
Time's Oriel
Waterslain
The Painting–Room
New and Selected Poems 1965–1990

TRANSLATIONS

The Battle of Maldon and Other Old English Poems
Beowulf
The Exeter Book Riddles

AS EDITOR

Running to Paradise: An Introductory Selection of
    the poems of W.B. Yeats
Poetry 2 (with Patricia Beer)
The Anglo–Saxon World
The Oxford Book of Travel Verse

KEVIN CROSSLEY-HOLLAND

The Language of Yes

ENITHARMON PRESS LONDON
1996

First published in 1996
by the Enitharmon Press
36 St George's Avenue
London N7 0HD

Distributed in the UK and Europe
by Password (Books) Ltd.
23 New Mount Street
Manchester, M4 4DE

Distributed in the USA and Canada
by Dufour Editions Inc.
PO Box 7, Chester Springs
PA 19425, USA

ISBN 1 870612 37 X (paperback)
ISBN 1 870612 82 5 (hardback)

The hardback edition, which has been bound
by The Fine Bindery, is limited
to thirty signed and numbered copies,
each one containing a
handwritten poem from the collection.

Typeset in 10pt Bembo by Bryan Williamson, Frome,
and printed in Great Britain by
The Cromwell Press, Broughton Gifford, Wiltshire

for Linda, with love

Acknowledgements

Poems in this volume have first appeared in the following magazines: *Acumen, Agenda, Aldeburgh Festival Programme Book, Ambit, The Green Book, Illuminations, Outposts, Poetry Review, The Rialto, The Spectator, Summit Avenue Express, The Times Literary Supplement, The Walsham Observer.*

'Because' formed part of *Roy Lewis LXXX*, a festschrift for the eightieth birthday of Roy Lewis, published by the Keepsake Press & fellow printers (1993); 'Eleanor's Advent' was first published in a limited edition, with engravings by Alyson MacNeill, by the Old Stile Press (1992); 'Watercolour' first appeared in *The Sea*, an anthology edited by Peter Wood (David & Charles, 1994); 'Blue and Rising' was a contribution to *Bright Star*, poems by and about John Keats edited by Matthew Francis (Winchester City Council, 1995); and 'Two Nocturnes from *The Wildman*' forms part of the libretto of *The Wildman* (music by Nicola LeFanu), published by Boydell & Brewer (1995). The author is grateful to Peter Dale for his help with drafts of 'Portrait of a Daughter'.

'Anasazi Women' has been set and published as 'Song of the Anasazi: Soft Footfalls' for SATB divisi – a capella by Anne Kilstofte. 'Leaf-Girl' has been set by Donald Betts as part of 'Listening for Your Name: Images of Childhood' for soprano and piano; it has also been published as a poster-poem by Bernard Stone and Raymond Danowski at the Turret Bookshop. And the songs of the mother, father and Eleanor, with other words from 'Eleanor's Advent', have been set as 'Four Advent Carols' for SATB and organ by Stephen Paulus.

Contents

The Language of Yes

This world's wreckers are at their games
and everywhere it is late.

Words words words a fury of words
hype and shred and prate,
sanitise, speculate;
they please themselves.

How can I be content
with hollow professions
or the arm's length of the sceptic?
Even with the sensory,
the pig heart's slop-and-mess?

I still want.

Let me make and remake the word
which reveals itself,
unexpected, always various,

and be so curious
(affirmation's mainspring)
I sing the language of yes.

Blue and Rising

I have come to this resolution – never
to write for the sake of writing or
making a poem.   John Keats

White dust in my nostrils; my throat.
The track's a ribbon tossed over
the hill's back, and then it lollops
into a thicket. The only way in

to this seasoned log-cabin:
sprig of rosemary on my pillow,
acres of silence comma-ed by birds.
And now is the only place to begin.

'Your last words,' the green man says.
'Some were right, some wrong.
Bluebird? Never! And you knew it.
A false note for the song's sake.'

He strokes his Minnesotan beard.
'And knowing is not understanding;
to understand still not to grasp
what gives a rising poem blue wings.'

Eleanor's Advent

Mother's Song for the First Sunday

Which came first: word or dream?
Silver shiver on a screen,
I prayed for you and you were born.

Dumpling dancing in my womb.
Long-armed, long-legged, little frog.
I prayed for you and you were born

And I am born a second time,
my saving child-of-Bethlehem.
You are my offering; my gift;
still my loving perfect stranger.

Let me light your first candle.

December 3rd

Condensation, freezing fog, English blur.
Smoky December, that's what Martial says.
She heard a blackbird sing, and saw it surf-
and-splash out of blazing pyracantha.

December 4th

She instals herself, draped in her duvet
or her winking cat. She inserts her thumb
and her presence settles us. Four-year-old
omphalos, the world spinning around her.

December 5th

How this story fascinates her! But what
if it should change? What if the wolf escapes
next time? She will not take her eyes off it
and asks me to read it again. Again.

December 6th

Some are fruit, some flowers. Her sister is
long-fingered fern, maybe water-lily.
But she's a compote – no, a macédoine:
mulberry and plum, mango, persimmon.

December 7th

Her mother's speckled kimono: *it's like,*
she announces, and falters, wordfishing:
like bubbles what frogs make. Then they grow up.
They all change into gorgeous butterflies.

December 8th

Seeing how we hurt ourselves, and hurt each
other, she neither quails nor questions why.
Wheresoever there's a wound, she bustles
forward, shining, and plants a flower in it.

Sister's Song for the Second Sunday

Miss Eleanor Edith Sarah:
she's horrible, my sister.

On walks she whines all the way:
my path my dog my one my my . . .

She makes you say, *'scuse me 'scuse me,*
and takes my toys to annoy me,

especially my doll. She always
wants to wear a dress, even on days

when there's ice. If I could teach her
to be good, I would for sure.

Let me light your second candle.

December 10th

First snowflakes and she snubs her nose against
the glass. Light. Wet. I say it won't settle.
In lieu of last year's mighty snow-woman,
she suggests we try for a snow-baby.

December 11th

Mother: I heard you reading to yourself.
Ellie: Yes, and I'm learning to read now.
Mother: That's good. Your teacher will be pleased.
Ellie: Don't be silly! She can read too.

December 12th

Ελévn: bright one, river eyes shining
and a comedian's long upper lip.
Lullay my liking, Eleanor sweeting,
traipser and trooper, my small lollipop.

December 13th

There is a third – her little sister – and
sometimes she cries out, always beginning,
never getting anywhere. At midnight
my lost wife sweeps from room to empty room.

December 14th

Why is Christmas, daddy? So I tell her
the good tidings: silly shepherds, wise men,
a star, a stable. And Christmas, I say,
is Jesus's birthday. *Don't say Jesus!*

December 15th

A damnation of rooks, and sky so pale
blue it looks almost breakable. There's rime
on the lawn, each blade bristling, delicate:
a dazzling page she writes on, step by step.

Father's Song for the Third Sunday

I saw your first breath, breathless.
On my palms I weighed you, weightless.
Your lying so defenceless armed me.
Hearing your first scream, I sang.

In England white with ropes of blossom,
or in December, in Judæa.
Like Joseph the carpenter.
Like any father, anywhere,

crying *my daughter, my daughter,*
ich freue mich in dir.

Let me light your third candle.

December 17th

Spillikins, Memory, and jigsaw race:
she wants it understood she'll win. And when
she does, intent and pink, rosebud mouth pursed,
her first thought is to console the losers.

December 18th

Today her red–gold sister is not here,
so she controls the air–space, costume–chest,
felt-tips, VCR. She pulls out her thumb!
Easy sunlight and she sails into speech.

December 19th

As she looks, she is: Baroque *puttela*
not to be misled or lightly shaken.
Little redeemer! We nearly called her
Rosamund. We could have called her Petra.

December 20th

More ribbon, more lace, more leaping colour:
ambassadress from the courts of summer,
wearing ripe cherries; wearing whole borders!
Gardens, she says, *are never quite cloudy.*

December 21st

Long-lost, new-found: carolling to herself,
she claims her first brother. Locks on to him
like a limpet. And sitting in his lap,
arms about his neck, wins him for ever.

December 22nd

Sickly-sweet cloud around the sugarbeet
factory; jaundiced sun; and a songthrush
plump on the path, eyes fixed on kingdom come:
the most beautiful bird in the whole world.

Eleanor's Song for the Fourth Sunday

I saw a shooting star tonight.
    Christmas in the air!
And Jesus' birthday is tomorrow
    – what dress can I wear?
I'll sing, I'll kiss him when he cries,
    I'll brush his baby hair;
I'll bake him a birthday cake,
    and teach him a prayer.
I'll say thank you for having me.
    But... will he be there?

Let me light your fourth candle.

December 24th

Her quiet diligence is motherly,
her devotion Marian: unaware
she is aware of the power of love
entire. Amor! Quam dulcis est amor!

Envoi

And so she springs her box of days: hours past
and time to come. Jack Frost gnaws at the panes
but in her room a peacock stirs, flutters
to the Christmas light: momentary and sweet.

Still Life:
Eleanor with Field-Flowers

At last the bones. After
the blazing through flame-
haired nettles, so many,
such very brief stories.
For you I deciphered them:
a timeline entire, Craske
after Craske, gone topsy
and lichenous . . . taciturn
the black stone for the
foreigner . . . and Charlotte,
taken away, 5yr 3mo 4ds.

To forget; at last to be
half-forgotten. But one,
a sailor-boy shipped home
from Crimea, was restrained
still with pale flowers.
and you, 5yr and 3mo too,
that much and a dozen days,
were so quick to protest
on this level ground at
such a show of inequity.

Lifting a double fistful
and kicking up your heels,
you ran Craske to Craske,
pelting them with stars.
One bloom tigerish and
burning at the feet of the
black Dane. You invested
each mound. To Charlotte
you came last and grave,
and hemmed her long green
surplice with rosy petals.

We did not leave the way
we came, but side by side
through parkland thronged
and breathless, along a path
quite shiny with usage. At
times you dawdled, at times
danced. Dew on the grass.
Butter light. You stooped
and pressed a field-flower
between our palms. Down to
the water: you led me out.

Leaf-Girl

Round and round the trampled
ground between the flaming
maple and the black walnut,
and out across the nickel rink
to the winter warming-hut,
round, round with bounds and
yells, skips and little rushes
you chased October leaves.

Curtsy, shout, leap and spin,
your pale face thin and hair
haywire, the best red-gold:
so you became the leaves
you caught. And watching you
I think I thought there's
some movement, some pursuit
best expressing each of us.

A Prayer for Jade

You crouching
            and eyebright
(who have an eye always
for the tiny and particular)

and over the blades
of your fine shoulders
jade combers
                stropped
and spitting
and with heaven-bellows
                    collapsing
into themselves

faint smile
            ginger tread
and you not quite
lifting the lid
of your long fingers
            on your secret
handful of transformations

maelstrom and mill
– spill over spill
                    spraying
you with amulets

    precious shower

and you unmoved
                    and still
half-bowed
intent on your fierce orisons

Portrait of a Daughter

I'll draw you, my daughter,
in the shade beneath the tree,
so quiet you hear the world's voice,
so still you sense its moment.

No girl-in-the-green in oak leaves
with a passion of grass for hair,
no Rosie-round-the-haystack,
no yearning, egocentric Ophelia.

I see your head and shoulders
and whole body, nerve by nerve,
a host of troubled children,
some bloated, some skeletal.

This girl gnawing at a wrinkled breast;
this boy bawling at the empty sky;
this lump on the slow road;
this cheated meal for flies;

this bundle jolting on a cart;
this bald head; this threshing heart;
this bone-cage; this wafer;
this baby; these planet eyes.

You sit so still, you listen
so intently for each dumb child.
How can I draw you not sturdy,
not becoming as you are

but made of nothing more
than empathetic, wailing air?
Crouching hunger and dismay,
resignation seem to become you

as, taking them into you
– these poor ones, lost little ones
with only their lives to lose –
you grow into your own care

beneath the tree in the gloom.
I see you in your slow dream
learning, preparing, already near
the maze of responsibility.

Flowers you plant in others' wounds
seed themselves in you
and, looking up at me, you shine:
'I promise you. I promise.'

Walking on Water

The first ragged frill
round the fringe of the lake
tinny and splintering before
you put half your weight on it.

The waterway itself
was still mulberry and slate,
it hadn't even started
to straiten round the dogged barges.

Ice-houses, lantern-bright,
and white hoods nosing out to them,
snowmobiles cutting
huge figures of eight:
all weeks and weeks ahead.

Yet this was the first
of the season's mysteries:
'Winter must come,
the pale sun will stand still.
Nothing we do or say,
no prayers our old mothers pray,
can quicken or avert it.'

Meeting, dry-mouthed,
at the water's edge,
breathless we talked too much,
we were so careful not to touch,
and stared aghast at each other.

In the blue hour
a flutter of snow
– no more than a dozen flakes or so –
the first November birds.

Then winter came where we stood:
teeth, traps, and fierce forecasts,
death-mists, sudden shinings.
But still we looked, still
we stared: the worst
of winter burned away
and it became so clear.

I could see the two of us
way out from this beginning;
in your gaze I saw us both
in our summer season,
hands linked, love-locked,
walking on open water.

Pearls and Diamonds

So the Queen of the North has lost her
baubles: pearlspawn, diamond scintilla.

In the sizzling cold little bundles
reel and stagger: the angels of the artists.
First they huddle in a scrum, then they
raise their arms and squeal, and stiffen
to fall back into the flowering snow.

The swimming moon rises and, like water-
carriers, lovers float through faded rooms.
They place tulips of white light, tall,
very slender, on ledges of high windows.

On the city sidewalks families blow
bubbles, and the dancers swarm and lift
– no colour, every colour. Then each
jewel catches night, it congeals,
goes dark and silently explodes.
'Look! Look!' Mica; precious dust.

More memory than presence, a woman
drags back her rhubarb velvet curtains
and traces patterns with a shaking hand:
pink peardrops, dazzling slabs, misty
blue teeth. Is Jack Frost the thief?

(And in the city margin, a literary critic
rubs his watering eyes: the Elders
in Chelm thought that treasure had fallen
from the sky; and at another time,
in another country, another queen
with a diamond incised syllables on glass.)

Spawn and scintilla. One man turns his back
on the revelations of the midnight city.
He lies on his bed, a stone on his stomach,
and dreams about the Queen of the North.
Her loss is legendary. On the cold
white page of his mind with love
he inscribes: winter-blossom; tears;
once and future seeds; merry dancers.

White Noise

Night swallows fumes from the mouth of the stack, and dusty knots
of creeper that half-covers the brick are sealed with ice.
Lowering your voice, you talk about fireflies, all kinds of owls,
dim creatures on the slimy bed that never swim, they reach and slide.
The standard first and then seven tulips long-necked in the window:
you turn off all the lights to hear the sound of falling snow.
All we hear at first are the animal sounds of ourselves
– our hearts' iambs, and blood whistling round our heads, our coarse
    breathing.
And snow that past midnight we scarcely see falling
except on an uptide, dancing on our window ledge, continues to fall.

Outside and shapeless, we shuffle like ancients block to block...
This wind's from the east: cottonwoods blossom, chastened cars
take the veil, and each cable fitting wears a busby and plume.
Motors and treads, party laughter on the doorstep, the tolling bell:
they're dampered like dreams, they sound like memories of
    themselves.
A muffler's laid over the whole huge engine of the city.

Immoderacy! I slip and drift, and believe we have no destination
and will never reach one, and that's only the beginning.
There is something white stars say to you
and you throw off all the night to hear the sound of falling snow.
As we walk the watches, still the underhum withdraws,
exhausts and conditioners, fans and vents withdraw
until in the hour before dawn there is this:
this almost nothingness;
you, floating;
the sound of silence deepening, which is white noise.

Airmail

When my words fly
to you
I want them fast
and fiery as cardinals.

And soft, I add,
immeasurably soft, straying
and resolute –
thinking of your parts
(your lower lip, for instance).

But more than resolute:
I want them indestructible.
Made of air, and
winging it;
made of shining steel.

Making Light

I

Pulsing and utter
as the blue heron riding

currents of air above
the rocking river.

How long I've looked.
I've looked so long for you.

II

We knelt to blossoms
in the golden hills,

and it was as it was
before we broke in two:

blue wings beating
made light of space and time.

Middle-Aged Lovers

They even chew the little knobs of gristle.

That the astounding bell should ring especially
for them! And the horrid baby bawling
through the wall could still be their own.

This world, they know, is terrible. Each
silvered leaf has *fortuna* written on it.

See how they smile conniving smiles.

They're like one spliced divining rod
– godlike, twitching, grateful and absurd.

First Promises

In the first rapids
    and the month of the lion
are faintnesses
    the travelling year
masks or reinforces,
    sharpnesses
the growing flood
    wears or sweeps away,
and today not the charmless
    scent of the anemone,
not the muzz
    of my own shadow
nor the astringent
    knife of the wind,
simply the pale pink
    wrapping of the bud
growing in the darkness
    – the cone still
pointed as a skewer,
    very slightly sticky.
That and the exclamation mark
    of the beady nuthatch
as, head down,
    it walks at an angle
of ninety degrees
    from top to bottom
of the silent tree
    outside my window,
its insistent nasal thirds
    drilling pairs of holes
through the eggshell
    of my skull.

Almost forgotten
   in the months of the rose,
the grain and thunder,
   as year ripens
and dawdles
   with its sweetnesses,
these first promises,
   authentic, urgent,
vulnerable,
   given at a time
innocent of memory,
   and uncertain again,
even of spring.

Light Weather

To such a morning
muddied language (even the clod
of consonants) is inappropriate

– so are self-important passages,
unblinking owl-faces
and the god of the Old Testament.

Beside the island runway
the little springy aeroplanes
sniff the air.

Not a cloud in the sky,
and spry launches breeze
across the harbour

where circles and strings
of white buoys bounce.
This lick-and-spit's electric:

the lake water keeps opening
her pale hands
and flashing her secrets.

To such a morning
all our shortcomings
seem virtually redeemable;

disappointments are hung out to dry
and our shared history
is just a flawed first version.

High above the lighthouse
the ringed-bills are making
an open weave of wind.

The lake's blue shoulders
slope and bend;
I recognise this world is a sphere

and to the patient and persistent,
mindful of dream,
chance must come circling round again

on such a morning
as, flying out of winter,
you hurry to me here

and, on the island,
the willows and scarred cottonwoods
murmur in their buds.

Words-in-Bed

We need less than half this space!
Let's lay ourselves two levels deep,
or lie side by side, and close.
We'll confuse ourselves with sleep,
and when we wake no longer know
which tight word belongs to who.

Because

Across sodden socks of weed
and the limpid gutters. Across
the seethe around mossy outcrops,
Derwent pouring through small straits
permed by light; half-way almost
across the brawling water
where white wings and spray
seem to make headway back
upstream, a mule of a rock:

and more than half-way through
my life, with orange tips
and cuckoo-clocks, I'm back
again and pad along this easy bank
– still bent on getting out to it.

Counting Her Steps

She would still enjoy a head-to-head
with Heidegger, but not the waiting for it.
Her ardour for the sensual kept well in check
(say, chaste Lucy Rie) is no less pronounced
than it ever was, and her rejection
of the less than excellent uncompromising.
A gift for metaphor – and a sense
of humour. I can praise this woman!

But anxieties make her hoarse: her health;
the whole estate of her children. Her hair
is silver and ash, and downy as a cygnet.

Today she told me that on her constitutional
– and all day golden rods and storm clouds,
charcoal and indigo, and swirling leaves –
she counted her soft steps. One by one.
'Two thousand three hundred and ten,' she said.

True, she went on to ruminate on aspects
of the mile, beginning with the stride
of the centurion. But how easily she tires.
She sips and sups no more than a sparrow.
Is this how she begins to simplify:
counting and recounting the sum of her steps?

In Old Age

Glass this glass silvers:
With my left eye I see autumn.

With my right eye I see winter.
Bones my bones rattle.

I see autumn, I see winter.
Ah! If I were alive again.

Of Clay and Syllables, and Air

*In celebration of the life
of Dick Crossley-Holland*

not is
past tense

past time
and warm

tears are ours
this spring

and lemon
morning

Let us make a man from syllables.
I say his eyes will be sapphire blue.
You were going to say the same thing too.
I say like David – Michelangelo's –
he'll have long arms, long legs, big toes.
You praise his proportion: head, hands, feet
and say he'll make a fine athlete.
We can agree and disagree;
prediction is like this, and memory.
Let us make a man from syllables.

Let us make a mind, let us make a heart.
You say he'll do right and never great wrong.
I say he'll always sing the right song
or stay silent: what I call natural grace.
You say he will be brave, and face
all weathers with equanimity.
I say true teacher; kind; and witty.
You say a man who will love his wife,
his three children – who will love life!
Let us make a mind, let us make a heart.

And we will invest this man with air.
A subtle compound. I say he'll need
a mouthful – a sailor's daily creed
brought from mid-ocean. And you say smoke:
ring upon ring of Gitane, a blue cloak.
I say that mix of salt, iodine and mud
– let Nelson's air, Burnham air, sing in his blood.
Then may this creature of clay inherit
rushing breath: the holy spirit.
And we will invest this man with air.

        morning
        and lemon

        this spring
        tears are ours

        and warm
        past time

        past tense
        not is

Time Is, Time Was, Time's Past

There are so many ways.

At last, with a dog at your ankles.
Hopelessly pierced. Or in pieces.
Long after the positive test
– a donkey, or deadbeat, or doped.

First you spin on the Big Wheel,
then you walk over the top.
You die with a smile-and-scowl at your wife,
die in your cot or a dingo's jaws,
or maybe it's matches-and-necklace,
maybe your toenails are pulled out.

There are so many ways to go.

You set sail in a flame
or a foamy-necked floater;
you can travel by train to Rookwood,
you can cross with a coin on your tongue,

but sea-balloon or powder or stain,
soaring dark plume, ether:
you'll go. You'll have to go.

I saw an old fisherman
rigid at his wake – in one claw
his Meerschaum packed with black shag,
seven unbeatable cards
in the other. He was smiling
lockjawed at the amusements.

And I know of a woman
more meat than woman:
gang-banged and bound,
heaved half-alive
on to her master's spitting pyre.

How eager we are!
Body snatchers in the mire between
Front Lines; divers down to indigo,
befriending bloated corpses; pit-blasters,
mountain-rescuers. Today
we cut one wretched man
out of his concrete overcoat.

You'll go. We'll have you go.

We know the walkers
are waiting to accost us
on the beach and the bridge,
waiting in the graveyard, in dream,
at midnight – all the crossing places:

their left hands raised, their right hands
raised, quiet voices reminding us
of what is worse than the loss of senses
– skin, rain, song and sweet,
and the language of light:

even worse to be caught
in this world's closed circuit,
walkers, restless travellers,
trapped in time and howling.

From the Hall of the Autumn Prince

How can I stand the cicadas?
Raucous as the dead.

I see a silver needle of air
above my head.
It will spiral through my fontanelle.
I shall not go mad.

When . . . when I . . .
gristle in my throat.

When I become king
I shall legislate against the past
and sanctify the new.
The court will be convex
and I shall be surrounded
by inventors and babies.
As soon as a woman has suckled her firstborn
her nipples are to be shorn
– likewise the testicles of the father.

No one in the kingdom will be
as old as I am.

Bodies are to be burned,
ashes scattered.
Headstones will be forbidden.

How can I stand these cicadas?
I will have them netted and boiled,
all the dusty pines they squat in
are to be hacked down.

Do away with the sidling lizard
and its wicked ancient look.

I shall not go mad.

42

How many?
How many days?
There is shame in waiting,
the hot wind hisses
the same words again and again.

I will discriminate
against all likenesses
and comparison and memory.

Nothing is to remain of him.
Let the shrieking birds
carry him and his shade
out of the kingdom, high over the waters.

He is dead already.
This is the kingdom of the dead hand.
Hollowed steps, withered olives,
and all the little rancid shrines.
Husks of ritual.

I will do away with his foul dispensations.
He chokes on his own obsequies.

Cicadas. Cicadas.
I will keep my years young
with what's new and disposable.
I shall not go mad.

Scrape the ground clean of shards!
Roll out the shocking pink
when I . . . I

The Fox and the Poet

Please tell me please. How chancy is it
For a young fox to meet a hungry poet?

A poet! It's time you were properly versed.
Of all our enemies the poet is the worst.

Worst! I thought poets were just amorous,
devious and gaseous, penurious – but glamorous.

They're shape-changers. They dream and devour.
They translate you and take away your power.

Don't tell me please. If he catches me,
What will happen if some poet bandersnatches me?

You'll be locked behind words. Cribb'd; confin'd.
Howling you'll run to the limits of the mind.

Translation Workshop: Grit and Blood

Hige sceal pe heardra, heorte pe cenre,
mod sceal pe mare, pe ure maegen lytlad!
Word-stand, locking shield-wall
not to be broken down, nor even
translated in its own bright coin.
Courage, intention, resolve – won't do.
Out with Latinates! I want earth-words,
tough roots: grit and blood, grunt, gleam.

Harder heads and hearts more keen,
spirits on fire as our strength flags!
Here lies our leader, axed and limp,
the top dog in the dust. He who turns
from this war-play now will mourn
for ever. I am old. I'll stay put.
I'll lay my pillow on the ground
beside my dear man, my loved lord.

Alfred in the Alps

From Wantage. From Winchester. Under my tread the path unwinds.

Emerald and garnet and amber and jet. Upward, season-step. Pearl and swansdown. The stumbling king and his working men, his fighting men and praying men.

The immodest sun has shone for a week. He disarms the impossible peaks. He shouts at God himself.

The string-thin paths are crazed, the watercourses rusty and silent. Mountain-men we meet have skins creased and cracked as the skins they wear. My eye-balls ache, they're growing too large for their sockets.

But now at last the weather changes. I think we'll walk through clouds all day. Old habits. Dear unknowings.

I'll sleep, as I used to sleep, in the third hour after noon. And they'll tell me a butterfly danced out of my mouth. I will believe them.

I am of England. And I have cousins in Aabenraa and Brugge. I have friends in the Baltic and Arctic, where world's alphabet begins.

Chill days, dank evenings! The mercy of mood and change. My heart leaps with the eager orange-blue flames. Horses stamping. Woodsmoke tart and sweet.

Look at the shape-changers: dragon, sweet dancer, you cannot quite grasp them, ivory and oyster and lime and ash. Now they lift, and half-peaks soar and tumble.

I can hear my men tripping and cursing, finding their feet again. But they're climbing, still climbing: crossing the Alps.

South, the sun scarcely blinks, living is too easy. Vineyards. Misty purple grapes. And pampered men, impenitents, half-blind to the old imperatives.

Where's the true tip of the spear when oranges and lemons grow on the loggia?

My men should not go harvestless, my weeping women hungry; my little ploughchildren should not stiffen with cold. But some hardship's the best mulch. Give me high latitudes to grow spirit-fruit.

Think of the glory of the old oak. Listen to his painful story.

I'll wear this wrap of sopping mist. I'll watch this one dissolving crystal star. In this high wilderness, I do not ask for sight but to learn how to see.

Greece is ashes and Rome dust. There is no yesterday and tomorrow is too late. Lord, what is it you require of me this day?

The Viking Field

Not only thistles.

Gossamer: a shining network
woven before dawn.

Obstinate couch-grass
tall and blond
manning the ditches

and roses
tougher than they look,
craning their necks in hedgerows,
pale, shallow faces
following the sun's arc.

Scent of stone
and basting clumps of cow-dung.
Good warm glue.

A crinkle of silver foil
in the far corner.
Blind eye
flashing like a field of broken ice.

Day's breath bated.
Grass growing. The sound of it.
Sound of wool
growing on the lamb's back.

Systems of ants
stream out from their quarters
to inspect the field.

And even now
no dragons are forecast
for tonight,
but the candid sky
begins to congeal and sag.

Clover.
Wild garlic.
Ragged, unscrupulous crows.

Lance-leaves and heart-leaves,
tawny hairs, stinging.

Then all these spirit-wings:
this flickering assembly,
each silent woman flying
on her own,
double-headed axe.

The Old Monk: Valle Crucis

Under Fron Fawr
the wings of our old sycamore
whirligig again –
they're brittle and brown.

Huge carp skulk in the underworld.
The whole stew's alive
with glides and grins.

Saturday night
Brother Garmon and I
saw the floating bones
of Sister Linnet,
we heard her white skull singing.

Fron Fawr.
Almost half her green skin gone.
Purple for a season.

When I sit at this grille
the mass of the beetling hill
wholly occupies it.

Look at the sheep
perched on the escarpment:
dun and bright,
in and out of sunlight.
Look at the crown
and the rumbustious clouds

toppling over it.
I've grown so old and
it's halfway to God.

Scenes from Cathedral Life

1.   *King of the Isle of Man*

The warrior with knobbly knees lies dreaming
of felicity across the water.

He's almost closed his eyes trying to read
the graffito etched on his tapering waist.

His crouching lion raises his head and bares
his teeth at the unstained sunlight.

From somewhere lilac breath and so–delicate
pear blossom. Ah! If only he had a nose.

2.   *Higgledy-Piggledy*

Here are the higgledy-piggledy kings
and the queen bedded with at least one bishop

mocked by a quire of French adolescents
– all jeers and gestures and hoots and navels.

They're raised aloft, their tongues time-tied,
these men and women who stood on ceremony;

who sinned small sins in private and public;
whose worst nightmares never amounted to this.

3.   *Castrators*

Bishops are like rugby forwards . . . The ancient
impales us on his eyebrows: *Think* and *run?*

But you, Ann Vaughan, slender as a lancet
– or are you Miss Bodenham or else Miss Morgan

of Pen-y-Crug? – your eyes and lips, your brain
hammered flat, oak limbs buffed to a sheen...

And the Protestants, saving your presence:
systematic castrators of art.

4.   *In Time*

This world is grey-green: we could think
of lives as grilles of light beamed on to stone.

And what, we ask, is as moving as stories
of tolerant stone: steps scalloped by feet,

the head of the hound polished by fingertips?
On a swaying scaffold, the mason drills a hole

in what used to be St Michael's right elbow.
In time the patient prince will slay dragon time.

In Latter Days

After two or three
had gathered in His name,

the purring began.
Showers of bright semi-quavers
and the mountains skipped,
floods clapped their hands.

In the great emptiness,
on your knee-bones,
you dreamed about decay
and holy mildew
all over chiming England.

Again we sang;
then an officer trundled up
to the savage lectern
with his babyfood bible.

O ye gods...

Divine authority,
our fathers' cadences,
and their fathers' fathers,
shuffled off.

Committee-speak!
The work of the worthy
with flat feet,
fearful of fire and unknowing.

In the terrible gloom
you lowered your head,
accomplice
while the Word
was betrayed by the word.

The Aldeburgh Band

Somehow a mouth-organist
has got into the flue
of the gas stove in the Baptist Chapel.

Every minute or two
she draws a plaintive chord
that dies as the north-easterly
roars in the stack
and the blue flames leap.

But it's in the gazebo
painted star-white,
all the benches wet with mist and fret,
that I recognise what's happened:

when the timpanist plays hide-and-seek
and beats his tiresome tom-tom
in whichever cubicle I'm not,

I soon see or, rather, hear
the whole ragged band
is billeted piecemeal
around Aldeburgh.

So, for instance, the fat man
with the alpenhorn
has found his way into the massive
stone head of the sea-god –
Aegir, president of the flint-grey waves
– and he keeps bellowing in my ear
every time I pass him.

There's a pretty lutanist
behind that lattice window
on Crabbe Path;
whenever she leans out,
she runs her light fingers
along the modillion.

And the contralto with the treacly voice:
there's no escaping her!
She's always under sail, beating
up and down the windy High Street,
decked in globs of amber.

But where's the maestro
– some say magician?
Is he locked in the foundation
or under the long-eared eaves, still
tuning in?
The Aldeburgh Band:
did he have a hand in this?
Those who tell don't know.
Those who know don't tell.

Darkness comes in to land and I walk
along the beach
past the very last silent fisherman
with his lantern
and ghostly-green umbrella.
Crunchcrunch under my feet. Crunchcrunch.

Down to the water's edge
and still the music's everywhere:
all the strings night-bathing
and phosphorescent,
playing glissando;

the stray with the cor anglais,
lonely as a whimbrel
over dark water;

and far away,
far under the glagolitic ocean,
the now-legendary player
of the tubular bells.

**Footsore,
in Search of a Chinese Cellist**

Mouth leathers, heels blister
in fluttering Burwood
on the first day of spring:

she's not at St Mary's;
not at Uniting. Not even
the Church of Christ the King.

High in the dry palms
the cynical laugh
and bright parakeets sing:

Hey, man! You, mister!
What have you come for?
Where are you going?

I've come from the true north,
come to hear grace notes
and run round in a ring.

It's now or never,
and so it is never.
Tomorrow's the Boeing

over the outback,
muzak and movie, the body's
high shine and breathtaking fling.

Tongue-tied I had listened
while young woman old cello
fused and took wing –

thighs, elbow and bow,
chestnut and tight gut:
a new kind of being.

(Her teeth were jagged,
and her mouth a poor purse,
her ankles were Ming.)

Mouth leathers, heels blister,
and I've searched every church
for the girl from Beijing.

Not a wrist or a bridge,
not one note, not a haunt;
no, not even a quivering string.

The Second Attendant

No reason to exaggerate.
It was never the Queen of the Night
I saw in the hellhole
of Liverpool Street
but her Second Attendant.

The train she disembarked from
was sixty-five minutes late
(Intercity: drawn by Halley's Comet)
because she brought on a heart attack
in Carriage B
and then pulled the red chain.
Naturally.

Half-term holiday
and the previous train cancelled.
Passengers profuse and rank.
Well! as one man said,
at least the poor bugger
was spared the return journey.

As soon as the gang
in yellow hardhats spotted her,
they greeted her with wolf-whistles
and salvoes from pneumatic drills.
She conducted them
and laughed uproariously.

She was wearing a dress so black
it was green.

When she stooped
and fluttered the pretty red ribbon
two little children
couldn't resist her!
They dared the short cut over
the wet cement,
one wheeling the other.
She grinned and shook her head.

As for the stampede
and the ten thousand pools,
some gun-metal, some liverish:
child's play for this woman,
dressed as she was to kill.
The passengers could
scarcely take their eyes off her.
She made quite a splash!

And all this, she knew,
was just an overture.
Sky trembled.
Between high panes
the Dark Queen began to spit.

Arching her eyebrows, and far
from satisfied,
the Second Attendant
advanced on untold London.

Medicinal

Midnight boats: they're nuzzling
and saying something salty.
All our taverna tongues are one
and if I raise my voice it will
only bounce against that high rock.
Desolation! Once again I pray
I may strike water from it.

★

Respect is the first step.
Then I examine the lop-sided moon,
smell rain in stones, exchange
signs with a sweaty gardener-monk.
Obligation is the third step.
Faith is the fourth step.
Faith is the fifth step.

★

This poet! He didn't come in
at the door, and didn't fly in
through the window. The roofbeam
is secure, so how did he get in?
Monsieur! I am no architect
but I am physician. I insist:
for your condition, figure this out.

The Moon at Malaxa

Roots, cries sage
as soon as she sees him.
Remember your roots.

Then it's thyme:
you carry your own sickle
on your shoulder.

You'll fatten and drop
out of the sky,
says globe of dew.

And grave stone breaks
his vow: keep low;
stay nose-to-furrow.

Raising their eyes,
woman and man reflect
less body than spirit.

Hill clay holds
her breath, tightens,
cracks open.

How red dust rises,
sown with seeds
of silver light,

and each cell, singing,
reaches for him,
and aches.

Heavy Weather in Hintertux

Hunched over draughts on a chequer-board carpet,
oatmeal-rubbing, and glooming on the balcony,
ill-attuned to the idiocies of Radio Tirol
in the silly season: this is the sum of it.
Virgins in dirndls have limited charms.
It's down to the grotto and a long arm at kegel.
A bottle of obstler is the only quick way out.

Klammer and the ski-kings never showed up
and the Slavic trainers have squelched down
from the glacier. Cuckoo-mournful, cowbells toll.
Threading through ashen reaches and needles
– summer grazing, misty escarpments that
thrilled generations of poets and painters –
wanderweg and pfadspur clear their throats.

Deserters, departures! Out of this shining
cloud the butcher and his mutton wife go west
in their Mercedes, lean skis clipped to racks,
and the parkplatz looks quite cavernous.
Survivors become porous: sad containers
amongst the sopping hay-hedges, turning blue
with self-referrals, part of the place's lung.

Two Nocturnes from *The Wildman*

Song of the Nine Waves

Wave-roam, wonder-home –

Wind-push, moon-pull, breath upon breath –
Mother! Mother! Ploughed deep silver –
Cradle, cry-life-lane, gambolling grave –
Star-glass, summer-breast, furlong-leap, life-beast –

Wave-roam, wonder home –

Wild kiss to cancer, caress to kill –
Paws, spines, glitter-thistles, quartz blooms –
Sea-shift, shape-change, candid, spellbind –
Syllable, somersault, salt-glazed tongue –

The Tide, Rising

Drawn-dreep, shell-shine, heart's tide rising –
Rumouring, memory, sheenskin ripple –
Fingers, obsidian, asking all knowing –
Spark and spearflash, sea-serpent, hiss –
Gossip and knock, knock, wave-whack, plunge –
Rib to furrow, salt-surge, ocean-rut –
Overlap, overrun, overcome, undermine –

Watercolour

Our road: a winding flint-blue creek.
Ploughed fields a stiff, flashing sea.
The clouds are dun-and-purple mud,
Creeks and pulks awash with sky.

Notes on a Field-Map

in memoriam Cash Martineau

Corrugated and clouded,
many acres foxed,
face up in every season.

rookwing to mushroom

The Little Ouse still oozes
through Gallant's Meadow.
Fenced and throttled.

mushroom to muck

Badwell Hill Meadow.
Here I whistled Tempest
down the generous ride.

muck to chestnut

Bales of wild silk.
And the plump does
up-ending into their warrens.

chestnut to straw

Under light's blinding eye
boundaries, features,
characters all faded.

straw to chert

Here is Bull's Croft,
First Beeches. Second...
Felled. Gone to ground.

chert to pigeonwing

  ome   ado
This was Home Meadow.
Silver dust.

Coin

Last he looks
at the alien and sovereign
wheat,
air trembling over it,

then he turns
on his slow heel,

turns and goes

under the rainbow jets
spraying the beet

and what blindly he notices
are the backs of willow leaves
and their trilling,

and what he will remember
is well knowing

all that never now
can be harvested
beneath the sky's pale canyon

and he drives
and is driven

to the thousand-floringed sea

East, West

Pity the fool, poor frantic,
crossing himself over mid-Atlantic.

No time to win on either shore,
he's unable to give more than more.

He frequents apparent light,
and translates depth as height.

Looking east while looking west,
for each is better, and both best.

One End of Singing

Splitting stones
I open glittering ferric veins

and, scaling walls,
stare at cloud-formations over Wales.

The north-west caterwauling wind
strips the sea-terraced strand,

and sluices and trumpets
besiege Hurlstone's limpets

and try to shake them loose.
I want to learn what I can lose

and wear this sober suit of days
in which the word can grow wise.

I say I'll sing
this simplest song:

not what things signify but what they are,
each itself, each singular.

This is one end of singing:
back once more back beginning.

Anasazi Women

And with whichever story you come,
from whichever quarter or time,
the signs here mean the same.

Rock, clay, how they speak to us.

And as if from pink-brown pouts of cliff
snake-tongues of water
have slipped down, dripped down

and passing through themselves,
running through string-thin runnels,
the narrowest canyons of their own making,
grooved the high mesa, every limb:

skin-deep,
knee-deep,
thigh-deep,
hip-deep.
The passage of feet feet feet
rubbed away this white rock.

Women of clay,
sooty-lunged,
fingertips and palms
spiked by cactus,
how could they make these tracks?
Were they so blade-ankled
and slender-hipped?

Pots on their heads
heavy with hominy, pumpkin flesh,
were they so high-stepping,
knees to wasp-waists, each foot
placed directly in front of the other?

On this neck
high above the talus and twisted cliff-rose,
one petal of flint,
milk-white and deadly.
And look!
A sandal of crushed yucca leaves,
fringed at the toes.
Soft footfalls, fit for spirit-roads.

Women of clay, bearers of water.
Abalone in the sunlight.
Sweet song
of the wingbone of the golden eagle
crossing time.

And up top, as if the bandit wind
wields some giant rake with silver tines,
all the scruff and hardscrabble
is striated,
and scrub oaks rasp.
And where wrens flute
and loop,
the ground is stiff with sherds
– not sloping shoulders, slender hips,
not the little feet of dishes or fingerdips,

but all that remains
of pots proud-breasted and wide-hipped,
pot-bellied pots like melons and gourds,
ample, kind and porous.
Cream slip,
black slip,
orange on sepia,
mouth wide, womb-wide,
round as this poor planet
we make, and break.
How gently she rocks the globe
in her net of hair.

And the women:
bones of the women,
carters of corn and buffalo-fat,
hordes of gnats
gyrating around them:
all misshapen, ricked by arthritis;
their shining teeth
are ground down to their gums.

Neither tall nor slender,
not lanky as foal or fawn,
but thickset, short, stalwart:
poor imitations
of their own healthy pots.

Women of clay, Anasazi women.
High-stepping
through passage and cut,
crack and cleft
up and down from the windy mesa,
they left a dancer within warm rock.
Her feet tap, her fingers click,
time has not turned down her smile.

And there is a piper
lifting life's music,
replaying it to heaven.
Rock-woman, earth-woman,
coiled, almost foetal,
almost ready to spring out and stand,
singing-and-saying
and and and

Notes

Still Life: Eleanor with Field-Flowers.   Langham churchyard, Suffolk.

A Prayer for Jade.   A description of my daughter Oenone at Jade Cove, California.

Pearls and Diamonds.   A diamond-and-pearl tiara belonging to Queen Sonja of Norway was stolen from Garrards, the London jewellers (where it had been sent to be cleaned) during an armed robbery on 5 February 1995.

Light Weather.   Toronto, 1991.

Time Is, Time Was, Time's Past.   The title refers to Roger Bacon's Brazen Head. Rookwood: a cemetery in the suburbs of Sydney, Australia.

Translation Workshop: Grit and Blood.   The first two lines come from 'The Battle of Maldon' (lines 312–13). The second stanza translates them and the remainder of Byrhtwold's exhortation.

Alfred in the Alps.   This poem may owe something to George Barker's 'The Oak and the Olive'.

The Aldeburgh Band.   My Aegir, the Norse God of the sea, lives outside the house of the poet Herbert Lomas. I have renamed Crag Path after Aldeburgh's first famous poet.

Footsore, in Search of a Chinese Cellist.   Burwood is a suburb of Sydney in Australia. After hearing the cellist and her peers (all nationally known soloists, in Australia to learn English) play for pennies on Circular Quay, I went to Burwood hoping to hear them for a second time.

Two Nocturnes from *The Wildman*.   'dreep': drip.

Watercolour.   'pulk': marsh pool, small muddy pond.

Notes on a Field-Map.   Based on an 1842 tithe map of Walsham-le-Willows in Suffolk.

Anasazi Women.   The Anasazi were the precursors of the present-day Pueblo Indians of New Mexico and Arizona. Their culture lasted from about 100BC until Spanish missionaries, soldiers and settlers arrived at the end of the 16th century. 'mesa': table-land.